Food Field Trips

Let's Explore Chocolate!

Jill Colella

Lerner Publications ◆ Minneapolis

Hello Friends,

Everybody eats, even from birth. This is why learning about food is important. Making the right choices about what to eat begins with knowing more about food. Food literacy helps us to be more curious about food and adventurous about what we eat. In short, it helps us discover how delicious the world of food can be.

Chocolate starts as bitter seeds on the cacao tree. Adding sugar to cocoa beans results in something wonderful. It makes me think of ways that people can add sweetness, like kindness and generosity, to the world.

For more inspiration, ideas, and recipes, visit www.teachkidstocook.com.

Jill

About the Author

Happy cook, reformed picky eater, and long-time classroom teacher, Jill Colella founded both *Ingredient* and *Butternut*, award-winning children's magazines that promote food literacy.

Lerner Publications Company
An imprint of Lerner Publishing Group, Inc.
241 First Avenue North
Minneapolis, MN 55401 USA

For reading levels and more information, look up this title at www.lernerbooks.com.

Main body text set in Mikado
Typeface provided by HVD

Library of Congress Cataloging-in-Publication Data
Names: Colella, Jill, author.
Title: Let's explore chocolate! / Jill Colella.
Description: Minneapolis : Lerner Publications, 2020. | Series: Food field trips | Includes bibliographical references and index. | Audience: Ages 4–8 | Audience: Grades K–1 | Summary: "Introduce young readers to chocolate: how cacao grows, what a cacao farm looks like, and how cacao becomes chocolate. Simple recipes invite readers to work with this common treat."– Provided by publisher.
Identifiers: LCCN 2019046312 (print) | LCCN 2019046313 (ebook) | ISBN 9781541590366 (library binding) | ISBN 9781728402826 (paperback) | ISBN 9781728400198 (ebook)
Subjects: LCSH: Chocolate—Juvenile literature. | Cooking (Chocolate)—Juvenile literature.
Classification: LCC TX415 .C645 2020 (print) | LCC TX415 (ebook) | DDC 641.6/374–dc23

LC record available at https://lccn.loc.gov/2019046312
LC ebook record available at https://lccn.loc.gov/2019046313

Manufactured in the United States of America
1 - CG - 7/15/20

SCAN FOR BONUS CONTENT!

Table of Contents

All about Chocolate 4

Let's Compare 6

Let's Explore. 8

Let's Visit a Cacao Farm. . . 10

Let's Cook. 20
Let's Make 22
Let's Read. 24
Index 24

Picture Glossary

ALL ABOUT CHOCOLATE

Chocolate is made from cacao seeds. The seeds are ground up and mixed with sugar and sometimes milk.

Cocoa powder is also made from cacao seeds. It is used for baking.

LET'S COMPARE

Chocolate can be dark, milk, or white.

Dark is bitter. Milk is creamy. White is very sweet.

Some chocolate has added fruits, nuts, or spices.

LET'S EXPLORE

The story of chocolate begins on a cacao tree.

Cacao farms have many trees. Cacao trees need water to grow.

LET'S VISIT A CACAO FARM

Cacao fruit grows on the tree trunks. A cacao fruit is called a pod.

Pods change color as they grow. Many pods turn yellow or orange.

Do these pods look ready to be picked?

A farmer cuts a pod from a cacao tree.

Look at the pile of harvested pods!

How many different colors do you see?

After about a week, the pods are opened. Inside are white pulp and cacao seeds.

How many seeds can you count?

A pod can have between 20 and 60 seeds.

Farmers separate the seeds from the pulp. Then the seeds dry in the sun.

What else can the sun do?

Dried seeds are
called cacao beans
or cocoa beans.

The cocoa beans are ready to go
to a factory.

The beans are roasted, ground, and blended with sugar. This makes chocolate!

LET'S COOK

Always have an adult present when working in the kitchen!

HOT CHOCOLATE

Make the mix

INGREDIENTS

- 2 cups (250 g) unsweetened cocoa powder
- 1 cup (125 g) powdered sugar
- 1 teaspoon salt
- 1 teaspoon vanilla powder (optional)

1. Sift all the dry ingredients into a mixing bowl.

2. Whisk the dry ingredients until everything is blended.

3. Store the mix in an airtight jar.

Make a cup

INGREDIENTS

- 2 teaspoons hot chocolate mix
- 1 cup (250 ml) milk
- marshmallows, whipped cream, or other toppings (optional)

1. Pour the milk into a small saucepan. Have an adult bring the milk to a simmer over medium heat on the stovetop.
2. Add the hot chocolate mix to the milk. Whisk occasionally until the milk thickens, about 1 to 2 minutes.
3. Pour the hot chocolate into a mug and add your favorite toppings.

SEE THIS RECIPE IN ACTION!

LET'S MAKE

CHOCOLATE-COVERED PRETZEL RODS

INGREDIENTS

- 16 pretzel rods
- 16 ounces (450 g) chocolate, chopped
- sprinkles, finely chopped nuts, or other toppings (optional)
- wax paper

1. Put the chocolate in a microwave-safe bowl.
2. Have an adult microwave the chocolate for 30 seconds. Stir with a spatula.
3. Repeat step 2 until the chocolate is melted and smooth.
4. Dip a pretzel rod into the melted chocolate.

5. Place the pretzel onto wax paper. If you have toppings, sprinkle them over the chocolate on the pretzel.

6. Repeat steps 4 and 5 for the remaining pretzels.

7. Refrigerate the pretzels until the chocolate hardens. They will stay fresh for 2 weeks in an airtight container.

Let's Read

Fretland VanVoorst, Jenny. *Chocolate: How Is it Made?* Minneapolis: Jump!, Inc., 2017.

How Chocolate Gets Made
https://www.cbc.ca/kidscbc2/the-feed/how-chocolate-gets-made

Nelson, Robin. *From Cocoa Bean to Chocolate.* Minneapolis: Lerner Publications, 2013.

Nelson, Robin. *The Story of Chocolate: It Starts with Cocoa Beans.* Minneapolis: Lerner Publications, 2021.

NG Kids Makes Yummy Chocolate!
https://www.natgeokids.com/uk/kids-club/entertainment/general-entertainment/chocolate

The Story of Chocolate
https://candyusa.com/story-of-chocolate

Index

cocoa beans, 17–19
cocoa powder, 5
cooking, 20–21

dark chocolate, 6

milk chocolate, 6

pods, 10–15
pulp, 14, 16

seeds, 4–5, 14–17
sugar, 4, 19

white chocolate, 6

Photo Acknowledgments

The images in this book are used with the permission of: © 5bf5911a_905/iStockphoto, p. 12; © 8vFanI/iStockphoto, p. 23; © AND-ONE/iStockphoto, p. 6; © Anze Furlan/psgtproductions/iStockphoto, p. 19; © bedo/iStockphoto, p. 9 (cocoa pods on tree); © BestForBest/iStockphoto, p. 14 (cocoa fruit in hands); © bhofack2/iStockphoto, p. 22; © carterdayne/iStockphoto, p. 11 (purple pod); © creacart/iStockphoto, p. 20; © dimarik/iStockphoto, pp. 3, 11 (yellow pod); © Eliot76/iStockphoto, p. 15; © fcafotodigital/iStockphoto, pp. 3 (cocoa powder), 4; © Fedinchik/iStockphoto, p. 1; © Frankonline/iStockphoto, p. 16; © grafvision/iStockphoto, pp. 3 (cocoa beans), 17, 18; © Image Source/iStockphoto, p. 5 (boy); © JosephJacobs/iStockphoto, p. 9 (cocoa trees); © KreangchaiRungfamai/iStockphoto, p. 19 (cocoa beans roasting); © LanaCanada/iStockphoto, p. 8; © leezsnow/iStockphoto, p. 7 (box of chocolates); © M ROFIUL HAMDI/iStockphoto, p. 11; © Marina Usmanskaya/iStockphoto, p. 10; © Natalia_Grabovskaya/iStockphoto, p. 3 (sugar); © nerudol/iStockphoto, p. 5; © olaser/iStockphoto, p. 9; © Pascale Gueret/iStockphoto, p. 13; © PicturePartners/iStockphoto, p. 14; © Pinkybird/iStockphoto, p. 7 (white chocolate with nuts); © Prostock-Studio/iStockphoto, p. 5 (cocoa powder); © wmaster890/iStockphoto, p. 7; © Wojciech Kozielczyk/iStockphoto, p. 21.

Cover Photos: © BestForBest/iStockphoto (hands holding cacao pod); © carterdayne/iStockphoto (cacao pod in tree); © Fedinchyk Tanya/iStockphoto (various chocolates and chocolate candies); © malerapaso/iStockphoto; © PamelaJoeMcFarlane/iStockphoto (girl sipping hot cocoa)